WORKPLACE VOCABULARY
for ESL STUDENTS

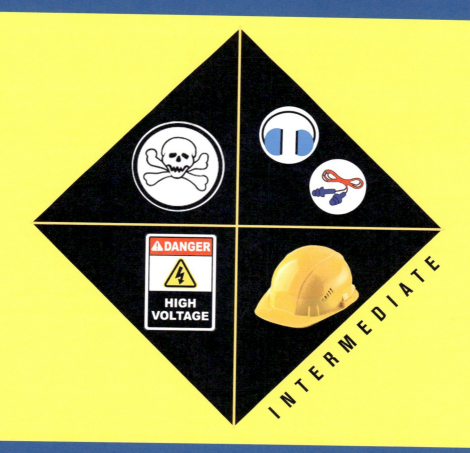

DANGER

HIGH VOLTAGE

INTERMEDIATE

WITH EXERCISES AND TESTS

G. DE GENNARO

AuthorHouse™
1663 Liberty Drive
Bloomington, IN 47403
www.authorhouse.com
Phone: 833-262-8899

Because of the dynamic nature of the Internet, any web addresses or links contained in this book may have changed
since publication and may no longer be valid. The views expressed in this work are solely those of the author and do
not necessarily reflect the views of the publisher, and the publisher hereby disclaims any responsibility for them.

Any people depicted in stock imagery provided by Getty Images are models,
and such images are being used for illustrative purposes only.
Certain stock imagery © Getty Images.

This book is printed on acid-free paper.

ISBN: 978-1-6655-1267-1 (sc)
ISBN: 978-1-6655-1266-4 (e)

Library of Congress Control Number: 2021900381

Print information available on the last page.

Published by AuthorHouse 09/08/2021

Workplace Vocabulary for ESL Students

TABLE OF CONTENTS

Unit I. Workplace Hazards

1. Asbestos

Where do you find it?

You can find asbestos at home and at work. Attic insulation and plaster ceilings in older homes have asbestos. Some insulation may fall inside the walls. There may be some asbestos in and around window and door frames, baseboards and around electrical outlets.

You can also find asbestos in the workplace. Building insulation is made from asbestos. Builders also use asbestos for floor and roofing tiles, cement boards, water supply lines and pipes, plaster, fireproof materials and textiles. Many building materials made before 1990 have asbestos. These materials are found in homes, factories, refineries, shipyards, vehicles, boiler rooms, elevators, cooling towers, electrical panels, HVAC duct insulation, vinyl sheets (for walls and floors), textured paints and coatings.

Why is it hazardous? Asbestos is made of tiny fibers. When workers drill, break, remove, saw or replace materials that contain asbestos tiny fibers are released into the air. If they breathe in these fibers they can develop breathing problems or cancer. It becomes a health hazard when workers breathe in asbestos fibers for many months or years.

Safety- People who work with asbestos must be trained and educated to work and stay safe. They must also wear protective clothing and use other safety equipment. When workers are trained, they learn how to recognize, handle and dispose of materials that contain asbestos.

Vocabulary

attic- insulation – plaster – baseboards - drill - refineries – cooling towers – textured paints – coatings - duct -equipment

1

2. Corrosive Materials and Liquids

There are many corrosive materials and liquids at home. There are corrosive materials in home cleaning products, drain cleaners, oven cleaners, bleach, rust removers, wax strippers and some laundry stain removers.

There are also corrosive materials and liquids in the workplace. Corrosive chemicals are used to manufacture fertilizers, dyes, paints, fabric colors, lubricants, metals, batteries, explosives and industrial cleaners.

Why are they hazardous? Corrosive materials and liquids are dangerous because they damage metals and other building materials. They are also very dangerous to people when they touch the skin and eyes. They are dangerous to the internal organs if they are swallowed. Corrosive liquids can burn, scar or destroy the skin and the internal organs. When workers are allergic to corrosive materials they can get dizzy or nauseous. If corrosive liquids get in the eyes they can burn them. Workers can also become blind if these materials touch their eyes. When workers breathe in vapors from corrosive chemicals they can have serious breathing or lung problems.

Safety- Employers have specific areas at work where corrosive materials are stored. Workers should always follow employer and other safety guidelines. When they work with corrosive materials they should wear protective equipment and clothing to protect their eyes, face, hands, feet and head.

Vocabulary

Corrosive - rust – strippers – stain -dyes - scar- dizzy -nauseous – damage – vapors- stored – vapors – guidelines – lubricants - fertilizers

3. Toxic Chemicals and Materials

Where do you find them?

There are toxic chemicals and materials at home and at work. They are found in paint, solvents, petroleum products (plastics), pesticides, glues, disinfectants, furniture, textiles, cleaning products and enamels. Chlorine, ammonia, carbon monoxide, asbestos and solvents are all toxic. There are also toxic chemicals in cleaning products for pools, bathrooms and kitchens, heavy duty industrial cleaning products, upholstery foam (inside sofas, armchairs, chairs and beds), cigarette smoke, pesticides, metal cleaners, nail polish, polish remover, car and truck exhaust fumes.

Why are they hazardous?
Toxic chemicals are poisonous to people and animals. They are toxic when people breath or swallow them. They can damage the stomach, liver and lungs; people can become very sick or die. Some toxic liquids and gases take away the oxygen from the air so people can't breathe. Workers can become drowsy, nauseous or dizzy if they breathe in toxic chemicals. They can also get cancer from some toxic chemicals. Some people are allergic to toxic materials. Toxic chemicals and materials can also be corrosive and flammable.

Safety
Workers who work with toxic chemicals and materials must be very careful. They must wear special clothing or equipment to protect them. When workers don't use these toxic chemicals they must store them in designated areas to keep everyone safe. All containers, lids, caps, must be secured properly. Toxic chemicals and materials at home must be stored away from children and pets, and away from heat and flames.

Workers who work with toxic chemicals must always follow company, employer and provincial safety guidelines.

Vocabulary

poisonous - pesticides – disinfectants – enamels – heavy duty – upholstery foam- polish – exhaust fumes – drowsy – faint – petroleum – allergic - flammable- carbon monoxide – sanitation - secured

4. Compressed gases

Where do you find them?

At home and at work, you can find compressed gases inside cylinders. There are compressed gases inside propane tanks, lighter fluid canisters, oxygen therapy tanks, gas cylinders, fire extinguishers, hairspray cans and computer and keyboard dusters.

Why are they hazardous? There is a lot of pressure inside cylinders and other containers that have compressed gases. They can burn or explode. Some compressed gases are corrosive. They can burn the skin or other body parts. Some compressed gases can corrode metals; others are toxic. They can take oxygen away from the air and kill people and animals.

Safety- People who work with compressed gases must know the hazards of working with these gases. They should wear personal safety clothing and equipment and handle cylinders with care. They should keep cylinders standing upright and leave valve caps in place. Workers must transport cylinders with hand trucks. They must not drop them or store them near sparks, electricity or flames. Cylinders must be stored more than 20 feet away from cylinders with fuel gas. Workers must not store cylinders inside lockers because cylinders need air. Workers should always follow employer and provincial safety guidelines.

Vocabulary

Cylinders – propane tanks – lighter fluid canisters -tanks - pressure- compressed -fluid -therapy -fire extinguishers – keyboard dusters -pressure – upright – valve caps - hand trucks – sparks – lockers – corrode - sparks

5. Flammable and Combustible Liquids, Gases, Materials

Where do you find them? There are different flammable and combustible liquids, gases and materials. They are found in the home and at work. Some flammable and combustible products in the home are spray paints, rubbing alcohol, nail polish, polish remover, aerosol cans, cooking oils, cleaners, hair spray, bug repellents, deodorants, body sprays, fragrances and sunscreen. People also work with flammable and combustible spray paints, gasoline, paint thinner, turpentine, kerosene, diesel fuel, and waxes. Hand sanitizer, moth balls and petroleum products are also flammable or combustible.

Why are they hazardous? Flammable and combustible products are dangerous because they can start a fire. Flammable liquids can start a fire at normal temperatures. Combustible liquids can start a fire at high temperatures. This fire usually has thick black smoke that is toxic to humans. Flammable or combustible materials can become heated and start a fire when they are in contact with the air. Some of these materials are dangerous because they can burn for a long time.

Safety- When people work with flammable or combustible liquids, gases and materials, they must never smoke, light matches or flames. They should never store flammable and combustible materials at high temperatures. Workers should always follow employer and provincial safety guidelines for handling flammable and combustible materials safely.

Vocabulary

Wax -polish -fuel -sunscreen – moth balls - sanitizer- aerosol cans – bug repellents - fragrances – sunscreen – turpentine – kerosene -

6. Pesticides

Where do you find them? You can find pesticides in the home and at work. There are pesticides in bug sprays, insect repellents, ant, roach and mouse traps, garden sprays, commercial farm/orchard sprays, flea shampoos, flea and tick collars for dogs and cats, moth balls, weed killers, lawn care products, fungicides, pool cleaners and wood preservatives. Pesticides can be dry, liquid, granular, powder or spray. People who work with pesticides usually work in farms, agriculture, orchards, greenhouses, pesticide factories, nurseries, stores and veterinary clinics.

Why are they hazardous? Pesticides are toxic because they are made to kill insects and pests. They can be lethal. They are poisonous to humans, wild and domestic animals (family pets and farm animals). Workers can get very sick if they touch, swallow or breathe pesticides. Pesticides can burn the skin and irritate the eyes. They can cause severe headaches and make workers dizzy. People who work with pesticides absorb them through the skin or eyes. They also breathe in pesticides. Some pesticides are corrosive and flammable.

Safety – Workers who handle pesticides must always read the safety and storage instructions on the product label. Store and lock pesticides away from children and pets. Never store pesticides with food or medicine. When you have liquid pesticides at home always follow the directions on the label for proper disposal. Never pour them down drains or toilets because they can pollute the environment. Keep flammable pesticides away from heat, flames, sparks and furnaces because they can start a fire. Keep pesticides in their original containers (the labels have important safety information, and information about accidental poisoning). Always keep caps and lids tightly closed. Do not buy more pesticides than you need.

People who use pesticides at work must follow employer safety guidelines for proper disposal.

Vocabulary

severe – lawn -fungicide -chlorine -preservative – pests - absorb – fleas - ticks – greenhouses - irritate - trap – weeds- orchard - granular -severe -lethal -accidental – disposal -environment

7. Chlorine and Bleach

Where do you find them? You can find chlorine and bleach anywhere in the home, in the workplace, in schools and in public areas. People use chlorine and bleach to clean, disinfect and to make fabrics and laundry whiter. You can find chlorine in many cleaning and laundry detergents, pool cleaners, auto supplies and sewage products. You can also find chlorine in places where they manufacture paper products, plastic, medicines, paints, textiles, dyes and insecticides.

Why are they hazardous? Chlorine is a strong chemical. It both corrosive and toxic. Bleach contains some chlorine but it is less strong because it is made for home use. Both chlorine and bleach can burn or irritate the eyes and skin. Chlorine and bleach can make people very sick. They can have difficulty breathing if they breathe or swallow these products. Chlorine vapors can irritate and burn the lungs. Chlorine and bleach become corrosive when they are mixed with other chemicals or materials. They can irritate the eyes, throat and lungs. They can also fill the lungs with fluid. Chlorine and bleach are self-reactive chemicals; after some time, they can have dangerous reactions. They can release toxic fumes, corrode metals and pipes, or build up pressure inside containers.

Safety -Workers must never mix chlorine or bleach with other chemicals or cleaning products because they can produce toxic gases. People who work with pool chemicals must store them away from high temperatures or sunlight, and always keep them in well ventilated areas. At home, people should always store or lock chlorine and bleach away from children and pets.

Vocabulary

disinfect - sewage – insecticide - ventilated

Unit II. Personal Protective Clothing (PPE) and Equipment

1. Protective Face Masks

What are they? Face masks are made of fabric, plastic, rubber and other materials. They cover the mouth and nose of a person. There are ear loops that go behind each ear. Some masks have straps that tie behind a person's head. There are masks that are made of strong paper-like material. Some fabric masks can be washed.

Paper masks are disposable. People wear them once, then they throw them away. There are masks of different sizes and styles so workers can choose what is comfortable for them. They also choose what is best for their jobs. When a person wears a protective face mask at work he or she can breathe normally. Some masks are called **respirators**. Respirators are plastic masks that cover the nose and mouth, and sometimes the head, and they have filters that clean the air so people breathe in clean air.

Why do workers wear protective face masks? Workers wear face masks to protect the face. They need to protect the mouth, nose and eyes. There are different masks for different jobs. Some masks cover only the nose and mouth, and workers must wear protective glasses or goggles to protect the eyes. Some masks cover the entire face. When people work in dusty areas, they wear a face mask to protect the entire face from the dust. Some people wear a dust mask when they mow the lawn or work in landscaping areas because there are insects, flying grass, dirt and debris that can seriously hurt them. When people work on farms or in agricultural areas, they wear protective masks because there are pesticides and other hazards in the air.

Workers also use masks when there is very little oxygen in the air. These masks help them to breathe so they can work. There are other types of masks that people wear when they work with gases and toxic materials. They wear respirators or **gas masks** so they don't breathe in toxic gases, carbon monoxide, harmful chemicals, welding fumes and asbestos. Other workers wear safety masks because there are fumes, vapors from oils, debris and flying materials where they work. Building, construction, home renovation and maintenance workers wear protective masks when they build or repair roofs made from tar because tar has toxic fumes. People who work in automobile manufacturing plants use toxic solvents and spray paint. Face masks and respirators protect the lungs and keep workers safe.

Construction workers wear safety masks because they work in dusty areas where buildings are demolished. These buildings have materials with tiny fibers: asbestos, fiberglass and mineral wool. When these fibers are inhaled they can be hazardous to the lungs and overall health. People who do construction work must also wear protective masks when they sand, drill or blast materials like rocks and concrete. Flying rocks, sand, glass and debris can get in the face and eyes.

Many health care workers who work in clinics, hospitals or medical laboratories wear **surgical masks**. They wear them in areas that are disinfected or sterile. They also wear them in hospital areas where people are very sick or need surgery because they don't want to spread germs. They cover their mouth and nose to hold back droplets or splashes of saliva. People who work in health care also wear masks to protect themselves because they work with diseased and sick patients who can spread disease from harmful viruses and bacteria.

Vocabulary

loops- mow - sterile- droplets - surgery - mist – tar - demolished – drill – blast – debris - diseased

2. Ear Protection

What is it? People who work in places with a lot of noise wear **ear plugs** or **ear muffs.** Ear plugs are very small objects made of foam. Workers take these ear plugs and roll them between their fingers, then they insert them in their ear canals. They can find ear plugs in different sizes and types of foam or plastic.

Ear muffs are larger than ear plugs. Sometimes they are called **acoustic** ear muffs. There is a headband that holds two soft round ear muffs that cover both ears. The headband can be metal or plastic. The round earmuffs have foam inside. This foam absorbs noise.

There are different earmuff styles for different types of jobs. Workers can wear them with helmets and hard hats. They can also wear ear muffs with safety glasses and protective masks. There are different types of ear muffs for different noise levels.

Why do workers wear ear protection? Workers wear ear protection when they work in noisy areas or use noisy equipment or machines. Ear plugs and ear muffs protect them because they reduce noise. There are many noisy workplaces: airport runways where airplanes take off, manufacturing plants with noisy machines, construction sites where workers use power tools and machines (jackhammers and excavators), night clubs with loud music, landscape areas where workers use lawnmowers to cut grass and chainsaws to cut trees. Sometimes workers need to wear ear plugs and earmuffs when the noise is very intense. When they remove this protection, even for a short time, they are not protected. People can lose their hearing over time if they don't wear proper ear protection. To work safely in noisy areas, they should always follow employer and provincial safety guidelines.

Vocabulary

insert - ear canals - plugs - headband - absorbs - jackhammers – chain saw -lumber - power tools – landscape - reduce – excavators

3. Eye Protection

Safety glasses

Goggles

Eye Wash Station

What is it? Workers wear eye protection or **safety glasses** in different workplaces and for different jobs. When they work in places with steam or heat safety glasses don't fog up because they are coated with a synthetic coating that keeps them clear. They are also comfortable because they are made with light materials. Safety glasses don't break easily because they are made with strong and durable materials. They can have prescription lenses for people who need to wear regular glasses (prescription glasses) when they work.

Safety goggles cover a person's eyes and the areas around the eyes. They cover the top, bottom and sides around the eyes. Safety goggles stay in place with an elastic strap that goes around a worker's head. When workers must wear prescription glasses they can wear them under their safety goggles.

Eye wash stations are found in many workplaces. They have special water to wash or rinse the eyes. This water is called saline solution. The eye wash station sprays the saline solution in the eyes for fifteen minutes. Many work places have eye wash stations in designated areas.

Why do workers wear and use eye protection? Safety glasses and goggles cover and protect workers' eyes. They must wear them when they work with harmful materials, liquids and substances that can get in their eyes. There are eye hazards when people work with chainsaws, drills, buffers, polishers, hammers, and other tools. Flying sand, rocks, dust, wood, metal, cement and wood chips can be very dangerous if the eyes are not protected.

Welders and workers who work with molten metals protect their eyes with goggles or safety glasses. Eye protection is also used when workers use chemical liquids, sprays and acids that can splash in their eyes. These harmful chemicals can make people blind. When accidents happen, a worker can lose one or both eyes if he or she does not use eye protection.

Many work places also have eye wash stations. When a tiny particle gets in a worker's eye, he or she uses an eye wash station to flush it out. People also use eye wash stations when harmful chemicals splash in their eyes. Eyes are usually washed or rinsed for 15 minutes.

Vocabulary

synthetic – fog – coating - buffers – polishers – hammers – molten- welding – particles – designated areas -flush - rinsed

4. Head Protection

A head protector is called a **hard hat** or sometimes a **helmet**. Hard hats are made from rigid plastic. A strap goes under the chin to keep hats in place. Some hard hats have a small flashlight on top, and some are lined with padding. Some hard hats are colored so managers and supervisors can find people with different jobs. Some hard hats have company logos and labels with employee names. Many companies also put reflectors on hard hats. Reflectors make hard hats and people easy to see at night. There are hard hats with visors to protect the eyes. There are also hard hats that have ear protection.

Why do workers wear head protection? Workers wear hard hats to protect the head from injuries. They wear them when they work in areas where they could suffer serious head injuries. There are special materials inside the hats that protect the skull. There is a space between the hat shell and the skull. When an object falls or hits the hat, the skull is protected.

Hard hats protect people who work in areas with falling or flying objects (rocks, debris, building materials, bricks, ceiling panels, tools, heavy or sharp items). They protect workers when there are moving parts from machines. Hard hats protect people who may bump their heads on beams and pipes. They protect them in work areas with electrical hazards (power lines, wires) and outside in traffic areas. People also wear hard hats when they work in high places (buildings) and there is the risk of falling. People who work in construction, mining, oil & gas industry and warehouses wear hard hats and helmets.

When workers are out at night they wear hard hats with reflectors. It is easier to see night workers who have reflectors. Hard hats protect workers who are outdoors for many hours under rain, snow, hail, sun and heat.

Vocabulary

rigid – flashlight -logos- lined - padding -reflectors – shell – skull - blow – bump- hail – mining - strap - injury

5. Foot Protection

What is it? When people need to protect their feet at work, they wear **safety boots**. There are special safety boots called **steel-toe boots**. Steel-toe boots are very strong because they are made with durable materials. These safety boots have an aluminum or rigid plastic toe and anti-slip rubber soles. They are also made with waterproof materials like treated leather. These safety boots tie up with shoe laces and cover the ankles. They are usually lined with materials that keep the feet warm and comfortable. There are safety boots that are made with fire-resistant materials. Steel-toe and safety boots are usually black or brown.

Foot protection is also called: safety shoes, safety boots, steel-capped boots and aluminum-toe work boots

Why do workers wear foot protection? Safety and steel-toe boots protect people who work in areas where there are foot hazards. They protect the toes, feet and ankles from minor and serious injuries. There are different boots and shoes for different industries and jobs. Electricians wear safety boots with thick rubber soles. Rubber helps them stay safe when they work with dangerous electrical wires and power lines. Construction workers work with many hazards; there are sharp objects, nails, broken glass, screws, broken bricks, blades and knives that can injure their feet and toes. Foot protection is made to keep workers' feet safe because it is made with rigid materials and thick soles.

Steel-toe boots protect workers' feet when they operate heavy machines and equipment. Warehouse workers use and work around forklifts. They lift and carry heavy loads and equipment. They use dollies and carts with wheels to move heavy loads. These loads can fall on their feet. Forklifts and other machines can accidentally run over people's feet. Steel-toe-boots minimize impacts when accidents happen.

Forestry, landscape and farm workers walk on uneven surfaces where they can fall. They always wear safety boots to protect their ankles from falls, twists and sprains.

Many safety boots and steel-toe boots have soles that are made with anti-slip rubber. There are slippery floors in restaurants, cafeteria kitchens and food processing plants where floors have water, grease and oils. Non-slip soles protect workers from falls.

Safety boots help workers protect their feet when they work with corrosive or irritating materials, chemicals and explosives. They also protect workers' feet when there are very high or very low temperatures where they work.

Vocabulary

durable – laces – rigid- sharp- waterproof – soles- fire resistant - sprain - blades – uneven - minimize – impacts

6. Protective Clothing

What is it? Protective clothing protects different parts of the body. There are jackets, vests, coveralls, pants, aprons and sleeves. Protective clothing is also called **safety clothing.** It is made with strong materials. Sometimes these materials are coated with rubber or other materials that resist chemicals, oil, heat, fire, abrasion, water and wind. Some jackets have pockets, zippers and inside storage pockets for cell phones and keys.

When safety clothing is made for outdoors it is waterproof, it does not let water inside. It is also insulated with materials that protect workers when it is very cold. There are also safety jackets, pants and coveralls that are made for high temperatures. They are made with materials that don't burn easily or burn slowly. The materials are fire retardant. Some materials are natural, like cotton. Other materials come from chemicals; they are synthetic. There are safety coveralls that protect the entire body, they cover it from head to toe. Sometimes they are made from materials that can only be used once. People who work in areas with contamination from radiation, biological hazards or asbestos wear disposable protective clothing. Head-to-toe coveralls are often used with face masks and respirators.

Why do workers wear protective clothing? Workers wear safety clothing because they need protection from different hazards: fire, chemicals, sharp objects, chainsaws, corrosive materials, chemical sprays, heat, low temperatures, asbestos, radiation, water, germ contamination and biological hazards.

When fire fighters work there is the danger of fire and intense heat. They wear clothing that is made with fire retardant materials. When they are in areas with fire and intense heat their protective clothing will not catch fire or burn like other materials. The material burns slowly and stops burning when it is away from fire. People who work in the oil, gas and the petrochemical industry also wear fire retardant clothing. It is also called flame resistant clothing.

People who work with chemicals wear special protective clothing. This clothing is made with synthetic materials that give extra protection to people who have to clean up chemical spills. People who work in nuclear plants also wear this clothing to protect them from radiation. When workers remove, demolish or clean up buildings and materials with asbestos and mold they wear head-to-toe protective clothing and respirators to protect them from asbestos fibers in the air.

When people work on road construction at night, they wear protective clothing with reflective stripes so drivers can see them. When men and women work outside, on roads, in parks, or in places with very low temperatures, like freezer cells and meat lockers, they wear insulated protective clothing. The insulation makes the clothing warm and comfortable for people who work in rigid temperatures.

Protective clothing is very important for people who work in forestry, parks and landscaping. It protects them when they use leaf blowers and there is flying dust, fragments, and dirt. Some of this clothing is made with synthetic material that protects them if there is an accident with a chainsaw.

Vocabulary

reflective - abrasion – radiation – biological hazard – fragments - sparks – contamination - chainsaw

7. Hand Protection

What is it? Hand protection protects the hands when people are at work. There are other names for hand protection: **safety gloves, work gloves** and **industrial safety gloves**. Safety gloves are made with different materials for different jobs. They are made with natural and synthetic fabric. Many work gloves are made with strong leather. Leather is comfortable and very durable. Safety gloves have coatings that make them waterproof and fire retardant. Fire retardant gloves are made with special fibers that don't burn. Other gloves are lined with fleece for insulation. Insulation is used to keep the hands warm.

Many safety gloves have hooks or elastic closures for a secure fit. There are work gloves with touch-screen fingers so workers can use cell phone. Most work gloves are made with tough materials that resist abrasion and wear and tear. There are safety gloves with reinforced index fingers and thumbs. These gloves are also padded with foam to absorb shocks. Other safety gloves are coated to repel water and other liquids. Some safety, work and industrial gloves have reflectors for people who work at night.

Why do workers wear hand protection? Men and women wear safety gloves, work gloves and industrial gloves to protect their hands from hazards in the workplace. They can cut, scratch, bruise, puncture or burn their hands if they are not protected. They can also damage the skin with corrosive chemicals or they can hurt or break their fingers. Safety gloves are strong because they are made with tough, durable materials. They are made to protect hands and wrists.

When people work outdoors and there is water, snow and ice, they wear insulated and waterproof gloves because they need to keep their hands warm and dry. Insulated waterproof gloves are used by commercial fisherman, snow removal workers and cold storage workers.

People who work in warehouses wear safety gloves to protect their hands and wrists. They load and unload materials and objects that could hurt or cut their hands. Others who work on farms or agricultural areas, do general labor, work in construction, landscaping or forestry, need to use safety gloves to protect their hands from hazards like sharp objects, nails, wood splinters and rough surfaces. Work gloves are comfortable so people can work with them all day. There are gloves with rubber coatings that help workers grip tools and equipment.

Safety gloves protect hands, fingers and wrists because they are padded. They have reinforced thumbs, index fingers, knuckles and finger tips. People who do auto maintenance and repair heavy equipment, or do towing and transportation wear padded safety gloves because they absorb shocks and vibrations.

Workers who work in chemical laboratories or petrochemical plants need to protect their hands from harsh chemicals. Chemical liquids and materials, acid, solvents, gasoline, alcohols, chlorine, peroxide, oils and corrosive liquids can be very harmful if they touch the hands.

Fire fighters and welders wear fire retardant gloves because they work in places with intense heat and fire. These gloves resist high temperatures and slow down flames. They can save the lives of those workers.

Vocabulary

coatings – fleece – bruise – puncture - wear and tear – abrasion- reinforced – repel - padded – ribbing – vibrations – harsh - gear- splinters – knuckles

Unit III

Warning Signs

NO TRESPASSING

When workers see this sign, they are not allowed to go beyond the sign or this point. They are not allowed to walk or drive beyond the sign because it is dangerous on the other side. This warning sign protects workers and other people from dangers at work. People can also find this sign in public and private places.

HIGH VOLTAGE

This sign tells workers that there are electrical wires, power lines or industrial equipment with high voltage in the area. The power lines may be above where people cannot see them. High voltage is very dangerous because people can be electrocuted if they touch or go near areas with power lines. Electric shocks can burn a person's skin and internal organs. Electric shocks can also stop a person's heart. It is important to obey the warning sign.

EMERGENCY EXIT

When there is an emergency, this sign shows people how to leave a building or an area. Emergency exits take people outside so they are away from danger. These exits have hallways, doors and stairs that are clear so people can leave the area quickly. Large buildings with many employees and other people have two, three or more emergency exits. It is always good to know all the emergency exits in a building or work area before emergencies happen. Employers always show or tell employees what to do if there is an emergency. This is called *Emergency Evacuation Plan*.

FIRE EXIT

When there is a fire, workers follow the emergency or fire exit to leave a building and go to a safe place. People who leave a work place or a building cannot take the elevator, they must take the stairs. It is not safe to take the elevator when there is a fire. Employees must always follow the employer emergency evacuation plan. The emergency evacuation plan tells workers what to do when there is a fire. It tells them where to meet when they are outside. It also tells employees what to do if someone cannot go down the stairs or is hurt. Sometimes there are arrows on the floor or walls that show people the way to the exits.

FIRE EXTINGUISHER

Workplaces have fire extinguishers to put out fires. When buildings are large, there are usually many fire extinguishers. When workers see a fire extinguisher sign they can find a red fire extinguisher inside a cabinet that is covered with plexiglass. Extinguishers are used only for fires. There are extinguishers that workers and other people can use when there is a fire, and there are other extinguishers that are only for firefighters. There are different types of fires. Some fires start because there are electrical problems. Some start in the kitchen where there is cooking oil. Some fires start when chemicals burn. Workers must always follow their employers' guidelines for using fire extinguishers and other ways to put out fires.

BIOLOGICAL HAZARD

Biological hazards are also called *biohazards*. There are biological hazards where there is hospital waste, animal waste and droppings, sewage, germs (bacteria and viruses), mold, some harmful plants and insects. People can find this sign in places like hospitals and health care facilities, sewers, farms, cleaning and sanitation areas, food manufacturing plants, meat processing and intensive farming plants, forestry and landscaping areas. Biological hazards can make workers very sick. They can develop allergies or infectious diseases.

SLIPPERY SURFACE

A slippery surface is a floor or ground where there is water, oil or grease. Sometimes workers cannot see that floors are slippery because the danger is invisible. This sign tells people that if they are not careful they can slip or fall and seriously hurt themselves. There are slippery surfaces in many work areas. It is slippery when people work with cooking oils, grease and floor wax. It is also slippery when there is ice or water on the floor or ground. Sometimes it is difficult to see ice on the ground or floor. This warning sign helps people so they can walk carefully on slippery surfaces. In most work places where there are slippery floors and surfaces workers wear non-slip safety shoes or boots.

NO ADMITTANCE

This sign tells workers and other people that they cannot enter the area. When this sign is on a door, building area or section, people must keep out because it may not be safe or it may be private. Sometimes only a few authorized employees can enter. Employees with special training or people with written authorization are allowed to enter the area.

NO ENTRY

This warning sign tells employees that they are not allowed to enter. This sign may be on a door, entrance or area of a building or commercial plant. Workers may find it outside their work area or at the beginning of a street or parking area. Sometimes this warning is on one-way streets. When workers see this warning they must not enter with their car because it is the wrong way.

RADIATION HAZARD

Radiation warning signs tell workers, customers and other people to stay away because radiation can be harmful to their health. Radiation is present in many work places. Dentist and other medical offices have radiation because there are X-ray machines and CT scan machines and equipment. Workers can also find radiation where there are power lines, electronic equipment, furnaces and lasers. There is radiation in nuclear power plants and nuclear weapon plants. There is also radiation in mines where workers are in contact with uranium. Our bodies absorb some of that radiation. Radiation changes human cells and it can also make people and workers sick and give them cancer.

FORKLIFT AREA

This warning sign tells workers and other people to always keep their distance when forklifts are operating. People must be very careful when they are in this area. A forklift driver cannot see a person who is standing behind him. He also cannot see a person standing in front of the load that he is lifting because there is a blind spot. Forklifts move quickly, they need a lot of room to move around and they can seriously injure workers in the area. Workers and others must not stand close to moving forklifts. There are forklift warning signs in warehouses, shipping and receiving areas, construction sites, recycling facilities and dockyards.

NO SMOKING

This sign tells people that smoking is not allowed because there are flammable materials, liquids or chemicals in the area. Smoking can be dangerous because cigarettes can start fires in many workplaces and at home. They can start small fires, but they can become disasters. A single cigarette in the wrong place can destroy buildings and kill people. Cigarettes can cause explosions and chemicals to burn for many hours. People who find this sign must not smoke, light matches or use lighters when they are in this area. Workers and others can find this sign in and around commercial gas stations, where there is fuel, in chemical plants, explosives and weapons manufacturing plants.

NO FOOD OR DRINK

When workers read this sign, they must not eat or drink in this area. Food and drink can ruin equipment, supplies, materials and fabrics. Food crumbs can get inside computers, computer parts and keyboards. Food can also ruin books, files, documents and office supplies. In some places it is hazardous to eat or drink because food can become contaminated with chemicals, drugs, or germs and workers can get sick. Leftover food and sugary drink spills attract bugs and pests. Pest infestations can destroy areas and bring infectious diseases. Every work place has designated areas for eating. Employees can have lunch, snacks and drinks in designated areas: lunchrooms, cafeterias, snack rooms or break rooms.

DO NOT OPERATE

This warning sign tells workers that they must not turn on machines and equipment because there is a danger or a problem. Sometimes these machines are broken, other times they need maintenance. These machines and equipment must be kept off. Workers who turn them on and operate them could cause an accident, stop production, damage products or hurt other workers. In some situations this warning sign tells people that only qualified employees can operate a machine. Employers use this sign to keep everyone safe.

MAINTENANCE IN PROGRESS

Workers may find this sign on machines, equipment or areas of a building in the workplace. The sign tells them that a qualified person is working on the machine or equipment so that it can work properly and do its job. When workers find this sign on machines or equipment, they must not turn them on or use them. When they find the warning sign in areas of a building or workplace they must be careful because some areas are not safe when maintenance is going on. When workers and others see this sign, they must be careful not to disturb anything. *Caution* tells people to be careful.

OUT OF ORDER

When workers see this sign, they know that something does not work properly or it is broken. Workers can find the sign on work equipment, large or small machines, vehicles, tools, parts of a building, elevators, washrooms, sinks, doors or windows. When machines don't work because they are broken, they are out of order. When a toilet does not flush, or it floods, it is out of order. When an elevator stops between floors and does not move, it is out of order. When something in the workplace is out of order employees must not force it or try to make it work. They must not touch it until the OUT OF ORDER sign is removed.

HOT SURFACE – DO NOT TOUCH

Workers who read this sign must not touch specific surfaces. Sometimes only this sign tells them that there is a hot surface, because they cannot see it. There are many hot surfaces in the work place. Some are in kitchens, boiler rooms and foundry plants. They can find this sign near cooking ranges, toaster ovens, pipes, exhaust pipes and metal parts from machines or vehicles. Workers and other people who touch these surfaces can be seriously injured or burned.

LOCK OUT FOR SAFETY

Workers see this sign when dangerous machines or equipment need maintenance or they need to be repaired. When a warning sign is on a machine, it is locked and it cannot be used or turned on. There is no power or energy and only authorized workers may do maintenance or repair work safely. A supervisor, or someone who has authorization puts the sign on the machine or equipment. There is also a lock and a tag with the name of the person who locked out the machine. Only this person has the key to the lock. The lock out is for the safety of all employees, and for the employee who will do the maintenance. It has different steps and it is a safe way to do maintenance or repair equipment and industrial machines.

UV LIGHT - DO NOT LOOK DIRECTLY AT LIGHT

This sign tells people that there are dangerous ultraviolet (UV) rays. Workers must not look directly at this light for any amount of time. They must wear safety glasses or goggles when they are around UV light. UV light can come from the sun or from machines. It has dangerous radiation that can damage the eyes if you look or stare at it.

Appendix A

EXERCISES

Unit I. Hazards

1. Asbestos

Match the sentences on the left with the sentences on the right.

1. People who work with asbestos must be
2. Many building materials
3. Asbestos fibers are released when workers
4. Workers must also wear protective clothing and
5. Workers learn how to recognize, handle and

a. dispose of materials that contain asbestos.
b. trained and educated to work and stay safe.
c. use other safety equipment.
d. made before 1990 have asbestos.
e. drill, remove or replace materials that contain asbestos.

Choose Yes or No

1. Only new homes and buildings have asbestos.   **YES   NO**
2. People who are trained to remove asbestos do not need protective clothing.   **YES   NO**
3. Workers can remove asbestos when they see it. They need to ask their supervisors.   **YES   NO**
4. Many building materials made before the 1990s have asbestos.   **YES   NO**
5. It is safe to work with asbestos if you don't breathe.   **YES   NO**
6. Asbestos has tiny fibers that are released in the air.   **YES   NO**
7. Anyone can work with asbestos. They only stop when they feel sick.   **YES   NO**
8. Asbestos is used to make building insulation.   **YES   NO**
9. People who work with asbestos for many years never have any breathing problems.   **YES   N0**

Answer the questions and discuss your answers with a partner or with the class.

1. Where do you find asbestos?
2. Why is it dangerous?
3. How can workers and others stay safe when there is asbestos at home or at work?
4. How old is your home?
5. Do you know if you have asbestos in your home?
6. Do you have asbestos at work?
7. What does your employer do to keep you and other workers safe?

2. Corrosive Materials and Liquids

Choose the best answer; A or B

1. There are many _____ and liquids in the home.
   a. cleaning products   b. corrosive liquids and materials
2. Corrosive materials and liquids _____metals and other building materials.
   a. damage   b. are dangerous
3. Employers have _____ areas where corrosive materials are stored safely.
   a. Safe   b. specific
4. When people work with corrosive materials, they should wear _____ .
   a. clothing   b. protective equipment
5. Corrosive materials and liquids are very dangerous if you _____them.
   a. Scar   b. swallow
6. Corrosive liquids can burn or _____the skin.
   a. Destroy   b. allergic
7. Cleaning products, drain cleaners, oven cleaners, _____, rust removers, wax strippers and some laundry stain removers. They are in the home and they are corrosive
   a. Dangerous   b. bleach

Write the answers to complete the sentences.

1. Corrosive materials and liquids are dangerous because

    _____

    _____

2. In the home, you can find corrosive liquids or materials in these products

    _____

    _____

3. To safely store corrosive liquids and materials you must

    _____

    _____

Answer the questions.

Do you have any corrosive materials or liquids in your home? _____

Which ones do you have and why are they hazardous? _____

Where do you store them? How do you keep your family safe? _____

Do you work with corrosive materials or liquids? _____

Where are they stored?_____

Does your employer have safety guidelines for corrosive materials and liquids?

Do you protect yourself with safety clothing and other safety equipment? _____

_____

3. Toxic Chemicals and Materials

Choose the correct words to complete the sentences.

designated areas - protective equipment - stomach/liver/lungs -breathe - drowsy - flammable -oxygen – foam – heat/flames - industrial – pets/children – cleaning products - provincial

1. Toxic chemicals are found in bathroom _____.
2. The _____in your home sofa also has toxic chemicals.
3. Heavy duty _____cleaning products contain toxic chemicals.
4. When people breathe toxic chemicals, they can become_____.
5. Some toxic liquids or gases take away the _____from the air.
6. Then people and animals can't _____.
7. If toxic chemicals are swallowed, they can damage the _____
8. Some toxic materials are also _____.
9. Workers who work with toxic chemicals and materials must use _____
10. Keep flammable toxic chemicals away from _____.
11. Toxic chemicals and materials must be stored in _____.
12. People who work with toxic chemicals must always follow the _____ and employer's safety guidelines.
13. Store toxic chemicals, liquids and materials away from _____.

Match the words on the left with the meanings on the right.

1. Exhaust fumes
2. Disinfectants
3. Textiles
4. Pesticides
5. Flammable
6. Chlorine
7. Upholstery foam
8. Carbon monoxide
9. Safety guidelines

a. comes from exhaust fumes.
b. is something that catches fire easily.
c. is found inside sofas and armchairs.
d. come from cars, trucks, buses.
e. kill insects and other pests.
f. are also called fabrics.
g. give information about working safely.
h. is used to disinfect pools.
i. kill germs.

4. Compressed gases

Answer the questions.

Where do you find compressed gases?

_____

_____

Write 5 products that have compressed gases:

_____

_____

Why are compressed gases hazardous?

_____

_____

Write 5 ways to work safely with compressed gases:

_____

_____

_____

Choose YES or NO

1. It is OK to drop cylinders with compressed gases, but you must pick them up quickly.   **YES   N0**
2. There are no products with compressed gases in the home.   **YES   NO**
3. Workers must transport cylinders with hand trucks.   **YES   NO**
4. Oxygen therapy tanks do not have compressed gases, they only have air.   **YES   NO**

5. There is little pressure inside cylinders and containers that contain compressed gases. **YES   NO**
6. People who work with cylinders that contain compressed gases should handle them with great care. **YES   NO**
7. Workers can transport cylinders with their hands. **YES   NO**
8. Workers who work with compressed gases should always follow employer and provincial safety guidelines. **YES   NO**
9. Workers must store cylinders with compressed gases standing upright. **YES   NO**
10. Workers must store cylinders near sparks, electricity or flames. **YES   NO**

5. Flammable and Combustible Liquids, Gases, Materials

Circle the correct answer.

1. Flammable and combustible liquids, gases and materials are hazardous because
   a) Because they can melt
   b) Because they can start a fire
   c) Because they can be toxic
   d) B & C
   e) A & C
   f) A, B & C
2. Flammable liquids, gases and materials can start a fire
   a) Below normal temperatures
   b) At normal temperatures
   c) At high temperatures
   d) A, B & C
3. Combustible liquids, gases and materials can start a fire
   a) Below normal temperatures
   b) At normal temperatures
   c) At high temperatures
   d) A & B
4. These products are flammable or combustible
   a) Hand sanitizer and alcohol
   b) Petroleum products and moth balls

c) Glass and steel
   d) A, B & C
   e) A & B
5. People who work with flammable and combustible liquids, gases and materials can smoke
   a) Sometimes
   b) Always
   c) Never
6. Combustible and flammable materials can burn
   a) For one hour
   b) For two hours
   c) For many hours

6. Pesticides

Answer WHO, WHY, WHEN, WHERE, HOW.

Who uses pesticides? _____

_____

Why do you use pesticides? _____

_____

When do you use pesticides? _____

_____

Where do you use pesticides? _____

_____

How do you store pesticides? _____

_____

Put the words in the right order to form the sentences.

1. kill pests. and they toxic are insects Pesticides because to are made
2. safety read label. the storage on and product the Always instructions
3. their pesticides in containers. original Keep
4. with store Never food. pesticides.
5. medicine. not pesticides store Do with
6. granular, be can liquid, spray. Pesticides dry, or powder

Answer the questions.

1. **Why is it important to keep pesticides in the original container?**

    _____

2. **Why is it important to keep pesticides away from flames, sparks and heat? And why is it important to store them away from children and pets?**

    _____

3. **Why should you always keep caps, lids and containers tightly closed?**

    _____

7. Chlorine and Bleach

Match the sentences on the left with the sentences on the right.

1. People use chlorine and   a. eyes, throat and lungs.
2. Chlorine   b. corrosive when they are mixed with other chemicals.
3. Chlorine is dangerous because it   c. because it is used in the home.
4. Chlorine or bleach become   d. is a strong chemical.
5. Chlorine and bleach can irritate the   e. bleach to clean and disinfect.
6. Bleach is less strong   f. is corrosive and toxic.

Choose YES or NO

1. Chlorine and bleach release toxic fumes.
   YES   **NO**
2. You can store chlorine or bleach where there are children and, but don't let them touch it. **YES NO**
3. It is OK to store chlorine pool chemicals in the sun when you don't have storage space.
   YES   **NO**
4. It is safe to store chlorine and bleach in small closets or storage areas with little or no air.
   YES   **NO**
5. Sometimes it is OK to mix ammonia and bleach. Be very careful.
   YES   **NO**
6. You must not mix chlorine and ammonia.
   YES   **NO**

Answer the questions.

How do you store your cleaning products at home?

_____

Do you use chlorine at work?

_____

Why do you use it?

_____

Where is the storage area for chlorine?

_____

Unit II. Personal Protective Clothing (PPE) and Equipment

1. Protective Face Masks

Complete the sentence. Use the information on page ?

1. Workers wear a face mask to protect the_____.
2. Some masks cover only the nose and _____.
3. There are different face masks for different_____.
4. When a face mask covers only the mouth and nose, to protect the eyes a worker must wear _____.
5. Some face masks are called _____.
6. Respirators help people to _____clean air because they have filters.
7. Some workers wear _____ so they don't breathe in toxic gases, carbon monoxide, and harmful chemical vapors.

Circle the correct answer.

1. **Face masks are made of**
   a. wood and steel
   b. fabric, plastic, rubber and other materials
2. **Paper masks that are disposable**
   a. they can be thrown out
   b. they can be used many times
3. **Face masks are also called**
   a. washable masks
   b. protective face masks
4. **Respirators have filters that clean the**
   a. face
   b. air
5. **When a face mask covers only the mouth and nose, to protect the eyes workers must also wear**
   a. prescription eye glasses
   b. protective glasses or goggles

Match the job on the left with the hazard on the right.

_____1. Landscaping/mowing the lawn   **a.** tar, toxic fumes

_____2. Farming/agriculture   **b.** fiberglass, asbestos, mineral wool

_____3. Home repair/roofing   **c.** flying dirt, grass, insects

_____4. Health care/Medical   **d.** flying rocks, glass, debris, sand

_____5. Construction   **e.** pesticides, insects

_____6. Road construction   **f.** spreading germs, disease, viruses and bacteria

2. Ear Protection

Choose the correct words to complete the sentences.

> Hard hats – safety guidelines - protected – jobs- protective masks – safety glasses – noisy- ear plugs – noise levels - acoustic – reduce

1. Ear plugs and ear muffs protect workers because they_____ noise.
2. People must always wear ear protection when they use_____equipment or machines.
3. When they remove this protection, even for a short time, they are not _____.
4. Ear muffs are sometimes called _____ear muffs.
5. There are different earmuff styles for different types of _____.
6. People can also wear _____ with earmuffs.
7. People can wear ear muffs with _____ and _____ at work.
8. Workers can wear ear muffs and ear plugs with _____
9. To work safely in noisy areas, workers should always follow employer and provincial _____
10. There are different types of ear muffs for different _____

Write the answers to complete the sentences.

1. When you work in noisy areas **ALWAYS**_____
2. **NEVER** _____during work with noisy machines or equipment.
3. When you need to protect your ears, face and eyes, **ALWAYS** _____
_____
4. To work safely in noisy areas, workers should **ALWAYS**
_____

Answer the questions.

1. What are two types of ear protection? _____
_____
2. Why do people use ear protection at work? _____
_____
3. Do you use ear protection? Why and when do you use it? _____
_____
4. What can happen if you don't use ear protection at work?_____
_____

3. Eye Protection

Match the sentences on the left with the sentences on the right.

1. Safety glasses are comfortable because
2. Safety glasses don't break easily
3. Safety glasses can
4. Safety goggles cover
5. An eye wash station

a. has saline solution to wash the eyes.
b. have prescription lenses.
c. because they are made with strong materials.
d. they are made with light materials.
e. person's eyes and the areas around the eyes.

Answer Yes or No

1. An eye wash station is used to wash the eyes and hands.
   YES   **NO**
2. An eye was station uses saline solution to rinse the eyes.
   YES   **NO**
3. Eyes are washed or rinsed for 5 minutes.
   YES   **NO**
4. Eyes are washed when harmful liquids splash in a worker's eyes.
   YES   **NO**
5. When chemicals or acids splash in a worker's eyes he should never use an eye wash station.
   YES   **NO**
6. Workers use safety glasses and goggles so they can see better.
   YES   **NO**
7. Safety goggles only cover the eyes, not the areas around the eyes.
   YES   **NO**
8. Safety glasses can have prescription lenses.
   YES   **NO**
9. Safety glasses with prescription lenses cover the eyes, and the areas around the eyes.
   YES   **NO**
10. Workers who need to wear prescription glasses at work can wear them under safety goggles.
    YES   **NO**

Answer the questions.

1. **Do you wear eye protection at work?** _____
2. **What kind of eye protection do you wear?** _____
3. **How does this protection help your eyes?** _____
   _____
4. **Do you think it is important to wear eye protection when you work with materials and liquids that are hazardous to your eyes and vision? Why?**
   _____

4. Head Protection

Choose the correct answer.

1. Head protection for the workplace is called
   a. a hat
   b. a hard helmet
   c. a hard hat
2. Workers wear head protection to
   a. get protection from the sun when working outdoors
   b. cover and protect the hair at work
   c. protect the head from injuries at work
3. When workers are out at night, they
   a. wear hard hats to protect them from snow and rain
   b. wear hard hats with reflectors
   c. must be very careful because it is dark
4. There are hard hats with visors
   a. to protect the head
   b. to protect the eyes
   c. to protect the ears
5. When workers have reflectors on hard hats
   a. managers can find people with different jobs
   b. they don't need any other protection
   c. it is easy to see them at night

Answer the questions.

1. **Search the internet for jobs that require hard hats or helmets.**
2. **What do you see?** _____
3. **Which jobs need head protection?** _____
   _____

4. **How many types of hard hats or head protection can you see? Why are they different? How do they help workers protect their heads from injuries?**

_____

_____

_____

5. **What are the risks for workers doing these jobs?** _____

_____

5. Foot Protection

Write the missing words. You can find them on page X

1. When workers need to protect their feet, they wear _____
2. Steel-toe boots have a toe made of _____or _____
3. Safety boots and other foot protection are very strong because they are made with _____
4. Safety boots cover the feet and _____
5. Safety boots have _____rubber soles.
6. The color of steel-toe-boots is usually _____
7. Foot protection is also called_____

Choose the correct word to complete the sentences.

chemicals - machines- jobs- corrosive - foot hazards - industries – sprains - rubber - anti-slip - protect - fall – twists - run over

1. Steel-toe-boots protect workers when there are _____
2. There are different safety boots for different _____ and _____
3. Electricians wear safety boots with _____ soles to protect them from electric shocks.
4. Steel-toe-boots _____workers' feet when they operate heavy _____and equipment.

5. Safety boots help forestry workers who walk on uneven surfaces. They protect their ankles from _____ and _____.

6. Steel-toe-boots and other safety boots protect workers who work with heavy objects that can _____on their feet.

7. When workers walk on slippery floors or surfaces, they wear _____ boots.

8. Forklifts or other moving machines can accidentally _____ workers' feet.

9. Safety boots help workers protect their feet when they work with _____ or irritating materials and _____.

What are their jobs? How do safety boots protect their feet?

1. Job_____ Protection _____
2. Job_____ Protection _____
3. Job_____ Protection _____
4. Job_____ Protection _____

6. Protective Clothing

Choose YES or NO

1. Protective clothing protects workers only from the waist up.	YES	NO
2. Protective clothing and Safety clothing are the same thing.	YES	NO
3. Safety clothing can resist chemicals, fire, heat, abrasion.	YES	NO
4. When safety clothing is made for outdoors it is called *fireproof.*	YES	NO
5. When safety clothing is made for fire or intense heat it is called *waterproof.*	YES	NO
6. There are safety jackets, coveralls, pants, aprons and vests.	YES	NO

Write the answers to complete the sentences.

1. When you work around fire or intense heat you wear _____
2. When you work in cold or rigid temperatures you wear_____
3. When there are work hazards and you want to protect the entire body you wear

_____

4. When you work with corrosive chemicals you wear_____
5. When you work at night and you are out on the road you wear_____
6. When you remove, demolish or clean up buildings and materials with asbestos you wear

_____

Match the job on the left with the right protective clothing on the right.

1. Firefighter
2. Freezer cell/meat locker
3. Asbestos removal
4. Night worker
5. Oil, gas, petrochemical
6. Chemical spill clean-up
7. Outdoor workers

   a. waterproof protective clothing
   b. protective clothing with reflective stripes
   c. head-to-toe protective clothing with respirator
   d. chemical resistant protective clothing
   e. fire retardant protective clothing
   f. insulated protective clothing
   g. flame resistant protective clothing

7. Hand Protection

Answer WHO, WHY, WHEN, WHERE.

1. Who wears hand protection? _____

2. Why do workers wear hand protection? _____

3. When do workers wear hand protection? _____

4. Where do workers wear hand protection? _____

Write the missing words.

1. Hand protection protects the _____ when people are at _____
2. There are safety gloves that are _____ and _____.
   They resist water and fire.

3. Some gloves are made with strong _____. Leather is comfortable and _____

4. Some work gloves are lined with _____ for _____

5. Some safety gloves have a secure fit because they have _____

6. Insulation inside work gloves is used to keep the _____

Write the answers to complete the sentences.

1. Men and women wear safety gloves, work gloves and industrial gloves because_____
   _____

2. Fire fighters and welders wear fire retardant gloves because _____
   _____

3. Safety gloves protect hands, fingers and wrists because _____
   _____

4. People who work outdoors and there is water, snow and ice wear protective gloves because ____
   _____

5. People who work in laboratories or chemical plants need to protect their hands because_____
   _____

6. There are gloves with rubber coatings that help workers because_____.
   _____

7. People who work in laboratories or chemical plants need to protect their hands_____
   _____

8. There are work gloves that help workers grip tools and equipment because _____
   _____

UNIT III. Warning Signs

Read the warning, then choose the correct answer.

1. NO FOOD OR DRINK
   a. When workers see this warning sign, they must not eat or drink in the area. They can have lunch, snacks and drinks in designated eating areas.
   b. There is a NO FOOD OR DRINK warning sign on the cafeteria door.

2. NO TRESPASSING
   a. You are not allowed to drive your car but you can walk beyond the sign.
   b. You are not allowed to go beyond the sign.

3. HIGH VOLTAGE
   a. This sign tells people that there are electrical wires with high voltage. High voltage is dangerous sometimes and people can go in the area if they are careful.
   b. This sign tells people that there are power lines with high voltage. High voltage is very dangerous and people must obey the warning sign.

4. LOCK OUT FOR SAFETY
   a. When this warning sign is on machines and equipment, they are locked but they can be used if people are careful.
   b. Machines with this warning sign have no power. Only authorized workers may work on the machine, repair it or do maintenance.

5. EMERGENCY EXIT
   a. It is always good to know where emergency exits are in the workplace before emergencies happen.
   b. When there is an emergency, workers call their supervisors and ask them to explain the emergency evacuation plan.

6. FIRE EXTINGUISHER
   a. Work places have fire extinguishers to put out fires.
   b. Workers can use fire extinguishers when a pipe bursts in the building.

7. SLIPPERY SURFACE
   a. It is always easy to see when a floor or surface is slippery. Workers don't need this warning sign.
   b. Sometimes people cannot see that surfaces or floors are slippery. This warning sign tells people to be careful because they can fall and get hurt.

8. NO ADMITTANCE
   a. When workers and other people see this warning sign at work, they must not enter because there may be a danger or hazard.
   b. When workers and others see this warning sign on private properties like homes and buildings, it is OK to enter.

9. NO ENTRY
   a. When people find this sign on a street they can drive in any direction.
   b. This warning sign may be on a door or area of a building or commercial plant. It tells employees that they are not allowed to enter.

10. BIOLOGICAL HAZARD
   a. People can find biological hazards in hospitals, farms, sewage and sanitation areas.
   b. Biological hazards do not make people sick if they don't have allergies.

11. RADIATION HAZARD
   a. This warning sign is only for doctors, dentists and medical staff because they work with X-ray and CT scan machines that have radiation.
   b. Radiation is found in some work places. This warning sign tells workers and other people to stay away from certain areas because radiation can be harmful to their health.

12. FORKLIFT AREA
   a. This warning sign tells workers that moving forklifts can seriously injure them and others. Drivers cannot always see people standing behind or in front of them. Workers and others must be very careful and keep their distance when forklifts are operating.
   b. If a forklift driver can see a worker, it is OK to stand close to the forklift to talk to the driver.

13. UV LIGHT - DO NOT LOOK DIRECTLY AT LIGHT
   a. The sun has UV rays. UV rays also come from machines at work. UV rays are harmful to the eyes.
   b. It is OK to look or stare at a UV light, but only for a few seconds, or with glasses.

14. NO SMOKING
    a. When people see this sign they must not smoke, light matches or lighters because there are flammable liquids and materials in the area.
    b. One cigarette can start a small fire, but small fires do not destroy buildings or kill people.

15. DANGER - DO NOT OPERATE
    a. When workers see this sign, it is OK to turn on and operate the machine or equipment if they need to do maintenance.
    b. Workers who see this warning sign and turn or and operate machines and equipment can cause accidents and hurt workers or themselves.

16. CAUTION – MAINTENANCE IN PROGRESS
    a. When workers find this warning sign on machines it is OK to do maintenance on them if they wear protective clothing.
    b. When workers find this warning sign at work, they know that some areas may not be safe. They need to be careful.

17. OUT OF ORDER
    a. When something dos not work properly it is out of order.
    b. When something at work is out of order, employees must try it until it works properly.

18. FIRE EXIT
    a. When there is a fire in a building, workers must run for the elevator.
    b. When there is a fire in a building, usually workers are not allowed to take the elevator, they should take the stairs.

19. HOT SURFACE – DO NOT TOUCH
    a. At work, there are many hot surfaces that people cannot see. This warning tells them not to touch these surfaces or areas.
    b. Workers who touch hot surfaces cannot get burned because there is no fire.

Appendix B

Test Your Knowledge

I. Look at the picture. Write the name of the personal protective clothing or equipment.

1.

_____

2.

EMERGENCY EYE WASH

_____

3.

_____

4.

_____

5.

 _____

6.

 _____

7.

 _____

8.

 _____

9.

_____

10.

_____

11.

_____

12.

_____

II. Complete the sentences with the name of the personal protective clothing or equipment.

a. To protect your eyes at work you wear _ _____

b. To protect your hands at work you wear _____

c. To protect the feet at work you wear _____

d. To protect your head at work you wear _____

e. To protect your ankles at work you wear _____

f. To protect your entire body at work you wear _____

g. To protect your toes at work you wear _____

h. To protect your fingers at work you wear _____

i. To protect your face at work you wear _____

j. To protect your lungs at work you wear _____

k. To protect your ears at work you wear _____

l. To protect the legs at work you wear _____

m. To protect your thumb at work you wear _____

III. Match the danger on the left with the personal protective clothing or equipment on the right. You can have more than one answer for each danger.

1. Noise
2. Fire
3. Ice
4. Falling objects
5. Asbestos
6. Biohazard
7. Chemical splashes
8. Chainsaw
9. Sparks
10. Flying debris, dust
11. Fumes
12. Electrical shocks
13. Falling objects/falling from high places

a. safety gloves
b. hard hat
c. insulated boots
d. safety glasses
e. steel toe shoes
f. face protection
g. safety boots
h. protective mask
i. safety shoes with rubber soles
j. hard hat
k. protective clothing/ chemical resistant
l. goggles
m. flame resistant clothing

14. Heavy objects that fall
15. Toxic gas
16. Jackhammer
17. Uneven surfaces
18. Sneezes
19. Airport runways
20. Chemical splashes
21. Cars at night
22. Loading/unloading materials
23. Vibrations

n. respirator
o. surgical mask/face mask
p. protective gloves
q. respirator
r. surgical mask/face mask
s. ear muffs
t. eye wash station
u. reflective clothing/equipment
v. ear muffs
w. ear plugs

IV. Choose a, b, or c, and write the word to complete the sentences.

1. _____are poisonous. They can damage the stomach, liver and lungs if people swallow or inhale them.
   a. toxic chemicals and materials   b. flammable liquids   c. asbestos

2. _____ can start a fire at normal temperatures
   a. flammable liquids   b. chlorine/bleach   c. toxic chemicals

3. _____ are dangerous when they touch the skin and eyes because they can burn, scar or destroy the skin. They can also damage metals and building materials.
   a. compressed gases   b. corrosive materials and liquids   c. pesticides

4. _____ can start a fire at high temperatures.
   a. asbestos   b. pesticides   c. combustible liquids

5. There are _____ in bug sprays, insect repellents, garden sprays, commercial farm/orchard sprays, flea shampoos, moth balls and weed killers.
   a. compressed gases   b. flammable liquids   c. pesticides

6. _____is made of tiny fibers. These fibers are released in the air when workers drill, break or remove materials that contain _____.
   a. compressed gases   b. toxic chemicals   c. asbestos

7. You can find _____ inside cylinders like propane tanks, oxygen therapy tanks, gas cylinders and fire extinguishers. There is a lot of pressure inside these cylinders.
   a. pesticides   b. compressed gases   c. chlorine/bleach

V. What does the sign tell workers? Choose a or b.

a. Danger of radiation.
b. Do not go beyond this point.

a. Maintenance in progress.
b. Electric shock danger.

a. Run this way.
b. Emergency exit.

a. Run to the elevator.
b. Fire exit.

a. Compressed gases.

b. Fire extinguisher.

a. Radiation hazard.

b. Biological hazard.

a. Do not run.

b. Slippery surfaces.

a. Danger – no trespassing.

b. No admittance.

a. No entry.

b. Out of order.

a. Biological hazard.

b. Radiation hazard.

a. Moving forklift danger.

b. Forklift maintenance in progress.

a. Flammable materials.

b. No smoking.

a. Employee lunch room.

b. No food or drink.

a. Machine lock out.

b. Do not operate machine or equipment because it can be Dangerous

a. No admittance.

b. Maintenance on machines, equipment, building area.

a. Maintenance in progress.

b. Something does not work properly or it is broken.

a. Dangerous surface.

b. Do not touch, surface could injure or burn the skin

a. Lock out- UV danger,

b. Machine or equipment is locked out for maintenance or repair.

a. Ultra violet light danger to the eyes.

b. Radiation danger.

VI. Choose the best warning sign for each situation

1. A work parking area with one-way traffic:

a.

b.

2. A warning sign on a dentist's X-ray room:

a.

b.

3. An office building elevator is not working:

a.

b.

4. An industrial machine needs important maintenance. It is locked and there is no power so the employee who does the maintenance will not be injured:

a.

b.

5. A clothing factory supervisor wants to keep clothes and fabrics clean:

a.

b.

6. A hospital room is used to collect surgical and medical waste. There are infected needles, dirty bandages and used face masks. This sign is on the door:

a.

b.

7. A restaurant manager wants his employees to know that there is a fire extinguisher inside a glass cabinet on the wall:

a.

b.

8. A plant manager is working on an evacuation safety plan, he needs this sign:

a.

b.

9. Workers of a food processing plant work on floors that have oil spills and grease. Their manager does not want them to slip or fall and get hurt:

a.

b.

10. A supervisor wants only a few employees to an area of the building:

a.

b.

11. There are employees who work with lasers. Their supervisor has told them not to look at these lasers because they could damage their eyes and eyesight:

a.

b.

12. A warehouse manager wants employees and visitors to know that there are moving forklifts in the area:

a.

b.

13. A gas station attendant puts up this sign to avoid dangerous fires and explosions where there is gasoline:

a.

b.

14. A construction supervisor closed off a dangerous construction area. He does not want workers and others to get hurt:

a.

b.

Appendix C

Answers

Unit I. Hazards

1. Asbestos

Match the sentences on the left with the sentences on the right.

1. b.
2. d.
3. e.
4. c.
5. a.

Choose Yes or No.

1. **NO**
2. **NO**
3. **NO**
4. **YES**
5. **NO**
6. **YES**
7. **NO**
8. **YES**
9. **N0**

Answer the questions.

Answers can vary.

2. Corrosive Materials and Liquids

Choose the best answer; A or B

1. b
2. a
3. b.
4. b
5. b
6. a
7. b

Write the answers to complete the sentences

Answers can vary.

3. Toxic Chemicals and Materials

Choose the correct words to complete the sentences.

1. cleaning products
2. foam
3. industrial
4. drowsy
5. oxygen
6. breathe
7. stomach/liver/lungs
8. flammable
9. protective equipment

10. heat/flames
11. designated areas
12. provincial
13. pets and children

Match the words on the left with the meanings on the right.

1. d
2. i
3. f
4. e
5. b
6. h
7. c
8. a
9. g

4. Compressed Gases

Answer the questions.

Answers can vary.

Choose YES or NO

1. NO
2. NO
3. YES
4. NO
5. NO
6. YES
7. NO
8. YES

9. YES
10. NO

5. Flammable and Combustible Liquids, Gases, Materials

Circle the correct answer.

1. **D**
2. **B**
3. **C**
4. **E**
5. **C**
6. **C**

6. Pesticides

WHO, WHY, WHEN, WHERE, HOW

Answers will vary

Put the words in the right order to form the sentences.

1. Pesticides are toxic because they are made to kill insects and pests.
2. Always read the safety and storage instructions on the product label.
3. Keep pesticides in their original containers.
4. Never store pesticides with food.
5. Do not store pesticides with medicine.
6. Pesticides can be dry, liquid, granular, powder or spray.

Answer the questions,

Answers will vary.

7. Chlorine and Bleach

Match the sentences on the left with the sentences on the right.

1. e
2. d
3. f
4. b
5. a
6. c

Choose YES or NO.

1. YES
2. NO
3. NO
4. NO
5. NO
6. YES

Answer the questions.

Answers can vary.

Unit II. Personal Protective Clothing (PPE) and Equipment

1. Protective Face Masks

Complete the sentence.

1. face
2. mouth
3. jobs

4. protective glasses or goggles
5. Respirators
6. breathe
7. respirators or gas masks

Circle the correct answer.

1. **B**
2. **A**
3. **B**
4. **B**
5. **B**

Match the job on the left with the hazard on the right.

1. **C**
2. **E**
3. **A**
4. **F**
5. **B**
6. **D**

2. Ear Protection

Choose the correct words to complete the sentences

1. Reduce
2. Noisy
3. Protected
4. Acoustic
5. Noise levels
6. Ear plugs
7. Safety glasses – protective masks

8. Hard hats
9. Safety guidelines
10. jobs

Write the answers to complete the sentences.

Answers can vary

Answer the questions.

Answers can vary

3. Eye Protection

Match the sentences on the left with the sentences on the right.

1. D
2. C
3. B
4. E
5. A

Answer Yes or No.

1. NO
2. YES
3. NO
4. YES
5. NO
6. NO
7. NO
8. YES
9. NO

10. YES

Answer the questions.

Answers can vary.

4. Head Protection

Choose the correct answer.

1. C
2. C
3. B
4. B
5. C

Answer the questions

Answers can vary.

5. Foot Protection

Write the missing words.

1. foot protection – safety boots
2. aluminum – rigid plastic
3. durable materials
4. ankles
5. anti-slip
6. black or brown
7. safety shoes, safety boots, steel-capped boots, aluminum-toe work boots

Choose the correct word to complete the sentences.

1. foot hazards
2. jobs – industries
3. rubber
4. protect – machines
5. twists – sprains
6. fall
7. anti-slip
8. run over
9. corrosive – chemicals

What are their jobs? How do safety boots protect their feet?

Answers can vary.

6. Protective Clothing

Choose YES or NO

1. NO
2. YES
3. YES
4. NO
5. NO
6. YES

Write the answers to complete the sentences.

1. fire retardant – flame resistant
2. insulated protective or safety clothing
3. coveralls

4. safety clothing made with synthetic materials that resist chemicals/ protect people who clean up chemical spills
5. protective clothing with reflective stripes
6. head-to-toe protective clothing

Match the job on the left with the right protective clothing on the right.

1. e
2. f
3. c
4. b
5. g
6. d
7. a

7. Hand Protection

Answer WHO, WHY, WHEN, WHERE

Answers can vary

Write the missing words.

1. hands – work
2. waterproof – fire retardant
3. leather – durable
4. fleece – insulation
5. hooks or elastic closures
6. hands warm

Write the answers to complete the sentences.

Answers can vary

UNIT III. Warning Signs

Read the warning, then choose the correct answer.

1. a
2. b
3. b
4. b
5. a
6. a
7. b
8. a
9. b
10. a
11. b
12. a
13. a
14. a
15. b
16. b
17. a
18. b
19. a

Test Your Knowledge

Look at the picture. Write the name of the personal protective clothing or equipment.

1. Protective clothing/ Fire retardant
2. Eye wash station
3. Eye goggles
4. Safety boots, steel-toe boots, work boots, etc.
5. Protective clothing/ vest

6. Ear muffs
7. Safety eye glasses
8. Ear plugs
9. Face mask, respirator
10. Safety gloves
11. Hard hat
12. Protective clothing/coveralls

Complete the sentences with the name of the personal protective clothing or equipment.

a. Safety eye glasses, safety goggles
b. Safety gloves
c. Safety boots
d. Hard hat
e. Safety boots
f. Safety clothing/coveralls
g. Steel-toe boots
h. Safety gloves
i. Face mask
j. Respirator
k. Ear plugs, ear muffs
l. Safety clothing/pants
m. Safety gloves

Match the danger on the left with the personal protective clothing or equipment on the right. You can have more than one answer for each danger.

1. w,v
2. m
3. c
4. a,b,g
5. k,n
6. h,o

7. d,l,t
8. k
9. d,l
10. a,d,f,h,j,l,o
11. n
12. i
13. b,g
14. b,g
15. n,q
16. v,w
17. g
18. o
19. s,v,w
20. a,d,l,t
21. u
22. a,b,g,p
23. a,p

Choose a, b, or c, and write the word to complete the sentences.

1. a
2. a
3. b
4. c
5. c
6. c
7. b

- What does the sign tell workers? Choose *a* or *b*.

b, b, b, b, b, b, b, b, a, b, a, b, b, b, b, b, b, b, a

Choose the best warning sign for each situation.

1. a
2. a
3. a
4. a
5. a
6. a
7. a
8. a
9. a
10. a
11. a
12. b
13. b
14. a

References

Government of Canada, Canadian Centre for Occupational Health and Safety (CCOHS)

Province of Ontario Workplace Hazardous Materials Information System (WHMIS) Ontario Ministry of Labour, Training and Skills Development

Government of Ontario, Personal Protective Equipment guidelines

University of Toronto, Faculty of Environmental Health & Safety

Occupational Safety and Health Administration, United States Department of Labor

U.S. National Library of Medicine, National Institute of Health

Workplace Safety Insurance Board (WSIB) of Ontario

Food and Drug Administration (FDA)

Michigan State University Environmental Health & Safety

University of Iowa, Environmental Health and Safety

Disclaimer

This booklet is not meant to replace workplace safety instructions, provincial, state or federal guidelines, employer work practices, employee manuals or statutory guidelines.

Printed in the United States
by Baker & Taylor Publisher Services